D1443216

NATURE WATCH

NEW WORLD MONKEYS

Written by
Melissa Stewart

Lerner Publications Company • Minneapolis

CONTENTS

For Irene, who gave me the chance to see New World monkeys in their natural habitat

Lerner Publications Company
A division of Lerner Publishing Group, Inc.
241 First Avenue North
Minneapolis, MN 55401

Website address: www.lernerbooks.com

Library of Congress Cataloging-in-Publication Data

Stewart, Melissa.
  New world monkeys / by Melissa Stewart.
     p.   cm. — (Nature watch)
  Includes bibliographical references and index.
  ISBN-13: 978–0–8225–6765–3 (lib. bdg. : alk. paper)
  1. New world monkeys—Juvenile literature. I. Title.
QL737.P9S746 2008
599.8'5—dc22   2006101482

Manufactured in the United States of America
1 2 3 4 5 6 – DP – 13 12 11 10 09 08

Monkeys and Their Relatives

When someone says the word *monkey*, most people picture a capuchin like the monkeys above and on page 4. This is the small, agile monkey that they see at the zoo and that is pictured in wildlife calendars. One of these cute, furry monkeys appeared on the TV show *Friends*.

Most capuchins can be found in the tropical forests of Central and South America. They live in large groups and spend their days leaping from tree to tree in search of fruits, flowers, and other tasty treats. Sometimes they use twigs or rocks as tools to smash open nuts or catch insects hiding under a tree's bark.

All the while, the monkeys stay alert. If a capuchin spots a hawk or an eagle, it whistles sharply to warn the rest of its group. When a capuchin spies a jaguar or other **predator** lurking below, it urinates on its enemy. Then it jumps up and down, so dead tree branches fall and hit the predator.

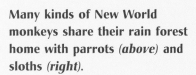

Many kinds of New World monkeys share their rain forest home with parrots *(above)* and sloths *(right).*

At midday, when the sun's hot rays beat down, capuchin monkeys stop to rest. Above them, brightly colored parrots call out to one another. Far below them, on the dimly lit forest floor, snakes slither among the leaf litter. The tropical woodland is always full of sound and activity. Even at night, when capuchins fall into a deep sleep, the forest is filled with the croaking of tree frogs, the gentle sweeping of bats' wings, and the quiet munching of three-toed sloths.

Capuchins are just one of the thirty-seven monkey groups alive today. There are four different **species,** or kinds, of capuchins. But some monkey groups contain as many as twenty different species. Scientists don't know exactly how many different kinds of monkeys share our world. So far, they have identified nearly two hundred species, but they are always on the lookout for more. More than twenty new monkey species have been discovered since 1990.

Most people don't use the terms *Old World* and *New World* anymore, but they did at the time scientists divided monkeys into two groups. Even though the entire world is the same age, many people used to think of the Americas as "new" because they were discovered more recently by European explorers. People thought of Europe, Africa, and Asia as the Old World because they had known about these three continents for many centuries.

Most monkeys live in the tropics—the areas just north and south of the equator. About half of all monkey species live in Asia and Africa. They are called **Old World monkeys**. The rest of the monkeys on Earth are called **New World monkeys**. They live in the Americas.

A few species of New World monkeys can be found in southern Mexico, but most live in Central and South America. Scientists believe that the first monkeys arrived in South America about 37 million years ago. At that time, the Atlantic Ocean was narrower and Africa and South America were closer together. A small group of African monkeys could have traveled from island to island and then drifted across the Atlantic Ocean on large clumps of plant matter. Those adventurous monkeys are the ancestors of all the New World monkeys alive today.

Chacma baboons live in southern Africa. Baboons are Old World monkeys.

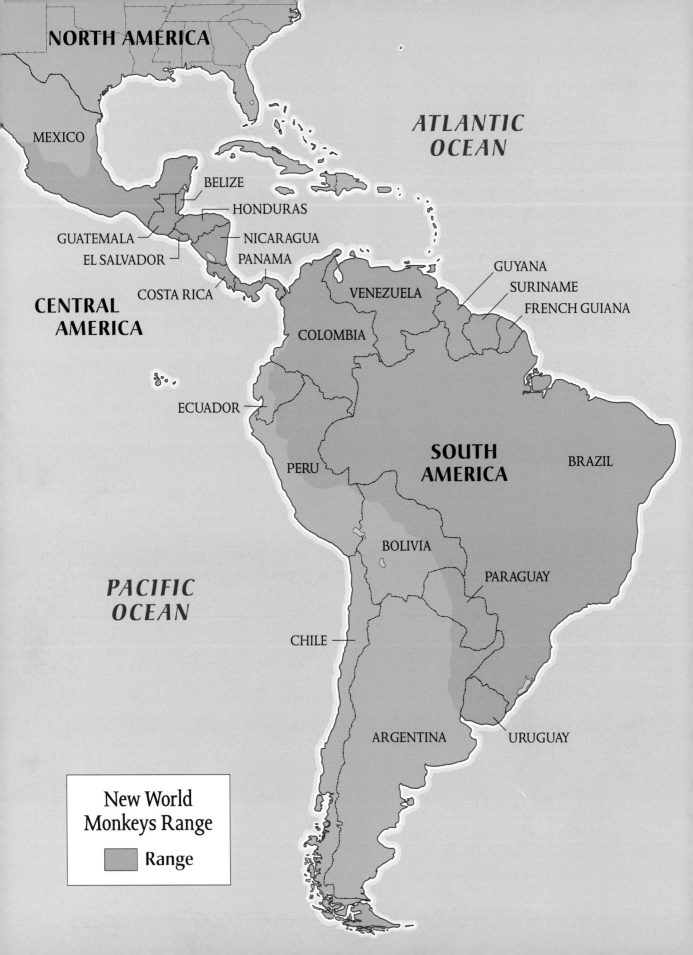

NORTH AMERICA

ATLANTIC OCEAN

MEXICO

BELIZE

HONDURAS

GUATEMALA — NICARAGUA

EL SALVADOR

COSTA RICA — PANAMA

CENTRAL AMERICA

GUYANA

SURINAME

FRENCH GUIANA

VENEZUELA

COLOMBIA

ECUADOR

PERU

SOUTH AMERICA

BRAZIL

PACIFIC OCEAN

BOLIVIA

PARAGUAY

CHILE

ARGENTINA

URUGUAY

New World Monkeys Range

Range

Both New World monkeys and Old World monkeys are members of an even larger group of **mammals** called **primates**. The first primates lived on Earth about 65 million years ago.

All primates have arms and legs that can move freely. Their fingers and toes are flexible. Primates also have forward-facing eyes that can judge distances accurately and large, highly developed brains.

But each group of primates has its own unique physical features and behaviors. They help the animals survive in their environment.

Most monkey mothers give birth to one baby at a time, and both parents spend a lot of time taking care of the youngsters. While the little monkeys are growing up, they learn important survival skills from the adults around them.

Mountain gorillas live in the mountain forests of Central Africa. They belong to a group of primates called the great apes.

New World monkeys are not the only modern primates that can trace their roots back to Old World monkeys. About 23 million years ago, another primate group called the **hominoids** evolved from the ancestors of Old World monkeys. As time passed, the early hominoids developed first into the great apes—orangutans, gorillas, bonobos, and chimpanzees—and then into humans.

New World monkeys spend almost all their time in the trees. They use all four limbs to climb, leap, and swing through the forest. Most New World monkeys feed on plants and insects during the day and sleep at night.

The smallest New World monkey, the pygmy marmoset, weighs about as much as a chipmunk and can fit inside a teacup. The woolly spider monkey is the largest New World monkey. It weighs about 30 pounds (14 kg) and is a little larger than a medium-sized dog.

New World monkeys have smaller bodies and broader, flatter noses that their Old World relatives. They are also

A baboon (*above*) is an Old World monkey. Old World monkeys have long, thin noses. Their nostrils are close together. The noses of New World monkeys, such as this marmoset (*right*), are wider.

A spider monkey holds onto a branch with one hand and its prehensile tail.

more active. Their powerful back legs, long arms, and hook-shaped hands are perfect for moving through the treetops.

Most Old World monkeys have **opposable thumbs**. Their thumbs are set opposite their four other fingers so they can grasp and hold objects. They have opposable toes too. New World monkeys have opposable toes, but not opposable thumbs.

Many New World monkeys have strong tails that can support the animals' weight as they hang from tree branches. The tails of some New World monkeys have a hairless **prehensile** tip.

The patch of exposed skin is as sensitive as human fingertips. A monkey can use it to grab and hold food or other objects.

Even though all New World monkeys have many things in common, there are also some important differences. Scientists divide the monkeys into two separate families based on the way they look and the way they behave. Marmosets and tamarins are very small monkeys with thick, silky, colorful fur. They have sprouting hairdos and elaborate ear tufts, mustaches, and whiskers.

While most monkeys have nails at the tips of their fingers and toes, marmosets and tamarins have long, curved claws. The claws are perfect for clinging to bark as the monkeys dash up tree trunks and scurry along branches. The 31 species in this family live in the tropical rain forests of Brazil, Colombia, and Panama.

All other New World monkeys—more than 60 species—are lumped together in one large family. Some people refer to this family as the prehensile-tailed monkeys, even though only some of its members have that special tail. The group includes the capuchins and their close relatives the squirrel monkeys. It also includes spider monkeys, woolly spider monkeys, and woolly monkeys. It has the noisy howler monkeys and the unusual-looking sakis, bearded sakis, and the uakaris. The group also includes the tiny titis and night monkeys. The monkeys in this family live in a variety of tropical forest **habitats**, and each group has its own specialized diet and habits.

A golden lion tamarin grips a branch with its long claws.

Spider monkeys can swing up to 40 feet (13 m) from one handhold to the next.

MARMOSETS AND TAMARINS

ALL THROUGH THE NIGHT, GROUPS OF MARMOSETS SLEEP huddled together in tangles of thick, lush vines. As soon as the first rays of sunlight appear on the horizon, the little monkeys shake themselves awake and fan out in search of food. Pygmy marmosets, like the one shown above, scurry to the highest reaches of the rain forest **canopy.** The larger, heavier marmosets stay a level below them, where the thicker branches can support their weight. Both kinds of marmosets are easy to track as they leap noisily from branch to branch.

Before the day is done, the little monkeys will have traveled about 1 mile (1.6 km) looking for food. They eat fruits, leaves, and buds as well as a variety of insects. To catch insects, a marmoset usually stalks and then pounces on its **prey.** But sometimes, it uses its long fingers to dig

Top: **Black ear-tufted marmosets feed on tree sap.**
Left: **A pygmy marmoset bites into a piece of fruit.**

A marmoset may also steal eggs from a bird's nest or capture lizards, frogs, or small snakes. The monkey pierces its prey's head with its long, sharp upper teeth. Then the monkey eats it.

The marmoset's favorite food is sugary tree sap. To get this treat, a monkey gouges a hole in tree bark with the tusklike teeth in its lower jaw. When the hole is deep enough, the tree springs a leak. Then the marmoset quickly laps up the sweet, sticky fluid.

As marmosets explore the forest, they occasionally stop to mark their path with a little bit of urine. Later, they follow the scent to find their way back to their sleeping spot. When the monkeys get thirsty, they search for water trapped inside flowers or curled-up leaves. The monkeys may also lick up dew in the early morning.

In the middle of the day, marmosets stop for a rest. Adults sprawl out on tree branches, and they **groom** one another. During grooming, one monkey picks insects, dirt, and bits of dead skin out of another monkey's fur. But grooming is more than just a way to stay clean. It is a way to build friendship and trust.

Not far away, a group of tamarins is resting too. Like marmosets, they spend most of the morning and late afternoon **foraging**, or searching for food. They eat many of the same foods as marmosets but in different amounts. Like marmosets, tamarins eat a lot of insects, but tamarins eat more fruit and less tree sap. Because tamarins do not have special lower teeth, they cannot gnaw holes in tree bark to reach the sap. But if tamarins spot a tree with cracks or holes, they will suck at the damaged areas and lap up whatever sap trickles out.

A gold-headed tamarin eats leaves and flowers.

Even though marmosets and tamarins have different diets, they have many things in common. They live in close social groups. These groups are made up of an adult male, an adult female, and as many as 18 youngsters of various ages. The group members often take time to play with one another, and they almost never fight. Marmosets and tamarins are the only primates that almost always give birth to twins. Sometimes they even have triplets.

When a new set of twins is born, the entire group helps take care of the babies. When the youngsters are hungry, their mother feeds them milk. But the rest of the time, their father is in charge. He carries them on his back when the group travels and watches them play while the group rests.

Older brothers and sisters also keep an eye on the little twins. If one of them spots a hungry predator, it sways back and forth and jumps up and down. The monkey drums on tree branches with its hands and makes deep rasping sounds. These actions let the other monkeys know that trouble is near. Then the entire group dashes higher into the forest canopy.

Twin cotton-topped tamarins cling to their parent's back.

Layers of a Tropical Forest

Canopy

Understory

Forest
Floor

Most scientists divide a rain forest into three layers—the forest floor, the understory, and the canopy. Different kinds of animals live in each layer. New World monkeys spend most of their time in the canopy. The smallest, most lightweight monkeys sleep and look for food in the highest parts of the canopy. Medium-sized monkeys move amongst the larger, sturdier branches near the lower parts of the canopy.

By the time the youngsters are about 6 months old, they can keep up with the group as it moves from place to place. They know how to find their own food. When the twins are about 2 years old, they begin to look for mates. Then they form new groups and start families of their own.

One member of the marmoset and tamarin group is a bit of an oddball. Unlike its relatives, Goeldi's monkeys usually have just one baby at a time. For the first few weeks of the baby's life, its mother provides all its care.

But then other group members begin to help out. They carry the baby as the group travels and watch it during the midday resting period. They share food until the youngster learns how to hunt insects and search for ripe fruit in the lowest levels of the rain forest canopy.

Goeldi's monkey family groups spend less time playing and grooming than other marmosets and tamarins. But they begin and end their days in the same way—safely nestled together in a dense tangle of vines.

Two Goeldi's monkeys share some food.

A white-faced capuchin stays alert to its surroundings. Capuchins, like those pictured above and at right, spend their lives in the forest canopy.

CAPUCHINS AND SQUIRREL MONKEYS

WHILE MARMOSET AND TAMARIN GROUPS SPEND THEIR nights huddled together, capuchins like to spread out. Just after dusk, each member of a capuchin group searches for its own sleeping spot. These monkeys prefer places where two tree branches meet, forming a cozy platform.

Each morning, capuchins wake up well before dawn and begin their daily search for food. Using their long tails, the little monkeys move swiftly through the forest's upper canopy in search of fruit, nuts, flowers, and leaves. Sometimes they also eat insects, small birds, frogs, lizards, and snails.

Capuchins are the most intelligent monkeys in the world. Scientists have observed them using rocks and sticks as tools. They have also learned that when they rub crushed millipedes on their fur, mosquitoes and other annoying insects stay away.

In the wild, every group of capuchins has a strong male leader. He is usually the largest and oldest member of the group. The leader protects his group against predators and shows the other capuchins the best places to find food.

A brown capuchin lifts a rock high off the ground to break a palm nut at its feet.

In the late 1970s, an organization called Helping Hands, Monkey Helpers for the Disabled began training capuchin monkeys to help people who are paralyzed or in a wheelchair. After several years of training, the monkeys can perform many important tasks for their owners. The monkeys know how to turn lights on and off, and they can pick up dropped items. They can flip the pages of a book, scratch itches, and retrieve the TV remote control. Some can warm up food in a microwave oven. They can even get a bottle of water out of the refrigerator, open it, and insert a straw.

"These little monkeys tend to form wonderful relationships with people," says Judi Zazula, the director of Helping Hands. "They also are very curious, and they love to manipulate objects. Those are the very skills that can help [people with disabilities] the most."

Above: **A young brown capuchin (*left*) watches an adult break open a palm nut.**
Left: **White-fronted capuchins use calls and facial expressions to communicate.**

At mating time, the leader gets to choose a female partner before the other males. Throughout the year, he is the one groomed most often by other members of the group. This is one way for capuchins to show their leader that they respect him. But capuchins also have other ways of communicating. They use facial expressions and body language to let one another know what they are thinking.

No matter where capuchins are or what they are doing, their close relatives, the squirrel monkeys, are usually nearby.

Squirrel monkeys aren't as intelligent as capuchins, but they have learned that if they follow capuchins, they're more likely to find food.

Squirrel monkeys live in groups with 20 to 40 members. They have yellowish brown backs with a paler belly and legs. The white, tufted hair on their ears and around their eyes makes them easy to identify. The constant chirping chatter of these playful little monkeys makes them easy to follow as they travel through the trees.

Squirrel monkeys spend less time grooming and socializing than capuchins. Some groups have a strong male leader, while other groups are ruled by a female. Many squirrel monkey groups have no clear leader at all. This may explain why they squabble and fight much more than other kinds of monkeys.

At mating time, male squirrel monkeys gain weight. Those extra pounds may help them during fights with other males. It may also help them survive if they are injured by another male and cannot forage for several days. The males fight because the winners get to choose mates before the losers do.

About 5 months after mating, the females give birth. It is the height of the rainy season, and sweet, ripe fruit is easy to find. This makes it easier for mother monkeys to get the extra energy they need to carry and care for their young.

Right: A squirrel monkey is feeding. It is hanging by its tail and resting on one foot. *Below:* Squirrel monkeys spend most of their lives high in the rain forest canopy. But once in a while, they come down to the ground to look for fallen fruit.

A young squirrel monkey crouches next to its mother.

For the first two weeks of a baby squirrel monkey's life, it clings to its mother all the time. The baby does nothing but sleep and feed on rich, nutritious mother's milk. Eventually, it learns to ride on its mother's back while the group travels. When the adults stop to eat or rest, the baby climbs down and wrestles with other youngsters or chases them through the trees. As the young monkeys play, they are learning skills they will need later in life.

If one member of the squirrel monkey group spots a snake or jaguar, it screams to alert its friends and family. Then all the monkeys release a nasty-smelling spray from scent glands on their bodies. It's usually enough to drive the predator away.

While male capuchins usually leave their group when they are old enough to survive on their own, male squirrel monkeys don't. Both males and females often remain in the same large, disorganized group for their entire lives.

A black-handed spider monkey stretches its long arms and legs. Spider monkeys, like those pictured above and at right, have long, strong limbs and prehensile tails.

SPIDER MONKEYS, WOOLLY SPIDER MONKEYS, AND WOOLLY MONKEYS

EVEN THOUGH SPIDER MONKEYS, WOOLLY SPIDER MONKEYS, and woolly monkeys belong to the same family as squirrel monkeys and capuchins, they look quite different. Spider monkeys, woolly spider monkeys, and woolly monkeys are larger and have longer arms and legs. They also have prehensile tails that make them masters of swing.

No monkey has longer limbs or a more powerful tail than the spider monkey. It can speed through the forest by leaping across broad expanses. Sprawling out—like a big, hairy spider—it can grasp a tree limb with its prehensile tail.

The spider monkey on the right drinks water from a balsa flower.

Spider monkeys live in large groups that sleep together at night. During the day, they break up into smaller groups called **bands**. A band usually includes several females and their young as well as a few protective males. As spider monkeys swing and leap through the tropical forest, they stop whenever they spot a tree with ripe fruit. Sometimes spider monkeys will also eat tender young leaves and other plant parts. And once in a while, one of them may grab and eat a nearby insect.

Spider monkeys can cover a large area in a short amount of time. When they are ready to release their wastes, they are far from the place where they found and ate the fruit. The fruit seeds aren't harmed by the animal's digestive system. The seeds pass through, land on the forest floor, and take root. Because they sprout far from the parent plants, the seedlings won't have to compete with the larger plants for light and food. As a result, they'll have a better chance of growing into new trees.

Most monkeys look for food in the early morning and late afternoon. They rest in the middle of the day to avoid the hot sun. Spider monkeys have a different eating schedule. They feed greedily all morning, then take the rest of the day off.

In the afternoon, the adults take turns grooming one another. The young monkeys spend their time playing. Sometimes their mothers join them for a game of hide-and-seek or tag.

These friendly, fun-loving monkeys often kiss when they meet one another, and they like to clown around. But they always stay alert. When spider monkeys sense danger, they bark like terriers and shake branches with their hands and feet. Sometimes they break tree branches and throw them at intruders. When the danger has passed, the spider monkeys return to their laid-back ways.

Unlike squirrel monkeys, male spider monkeys rarely fight at mating time. About 7 months after a couple pairs up, the female gives birth to a single baby. Spider monkeys develop more slowly than other kinds of New World monkeys. The mothers feed and carry their babies for 6 to 8 months. It is not unusual for a youngster to stay close to its mother for up to 3 years. Although the male monkeys are always close by, they don't help much with the babies.

When young female spider monkeys are old enough to survive on their own, they leave their band and join a new group. Some males stay with their band for their entire lives, while others wander off on their own.

Woolly spider monkeys look similar to spider monkeys. But the woolly spider monkey's fur is much thicker and heavier. They are also a bit larger and heavier than spider monkeys. This makes them the largest New World primates.

Right: **A baby black spider monkey sits close to its mother. Another adult helps watch for danger.**
Below: **A young black-handed spider monkey lives on its mother's milk for the first 2 years of its life.**

Woolly spider monkeys, or muriquis, are the largest primates in the New World. They are playful and affectionate toward one another.

During the hot summer, these monkeys, which are also called muriquis, begin to search for food just after sunrise. More than half their diet is made up of leaves, but they also eat fruit and seeds as well as some pollen and nectar from flowers. Muriquis rest for a few hours in the middle of the day and then forage again in the late afternoon.

During the cooler winter months, muriquis have a different routine. They sun themselves for a few hours in the morning and then begin to search for food. Instead of taking a break in the middle of the day, they continue to forage until about an hour before sunset.

Muriquis don't spend much time grooming one another, but they have other ways of expressing their affection. They greet friends and family members with hugs. Sometimes they suddenly stop whatever they are doing to embrace a nearby monkey—perhaps just to show they care.

A muriqui mother devotes a great deal of time and energy to raising her young. Most female monkeys produce milk for their babies for just a few months, but young muriquis are not ready for solid food until they are about a year and a half old. For all that time, the muriqui mother stays close to her youngster, providing food, care, and protection.

A muriqui is not able to survive on its own until it is 5 or 6 years old. At that time, young females join another band. Most young males stay with their parents' group and begin to look for a mate.

A young muriqui rides on its mother's back as she swings through the trees.

A woolly monkey mother also spends a lot of time caring for her young. She continues to feed her baby for up to a year and carries the little one everywhere she goes. At first, the youngster clings tightly to her belly, but when it gets a little older, it hitches a ride on her back.

Woolly monkeys are just as peaceful and friendly as spider monkeys and muriquis. They greet one another with hugs and kisses and spend several hours grooming every day. The rest of their time is spent napping or foraging in slow motion. Woolly monkeys are far less active than most of their relatives.

Like spider monkeys, woolly monkeys eat a lot of fruit as well as some leaves, seeds, flowers, and insects. An adult may eat up to one-third its body weight each day. That's a lot of food! A child weighing 60 pounds (27 kg) would have to eat 80 hamburgers a day to keep up with a woolly monkey.

Woolly monkeys have strong prehensile tails, so they are good at swinging through the trees. But they can also walk upright on their legs, just like people. Sometimes woolly monkeys run along tree branches with their arms outstretched for balance. They can also come down from the trees and walk on the ground.

Like spider monkeys and muriquis, woolly monkeys have no natural enemies. They are too big for hawks or eagles, and they can move through the forest more quickly than jaguars or other large predators.

HOWLER MONKEYS

LIKE SPIDER MONKEYS, HOWLER MONKEYS, SUCH AS THE ONE shown above, are large and have strong prehensile tails. But what really sets howlers apart from their relatives is the noise they make every morning.

As soon as howlers wake up, they gather in groups, climb to the top of the rain forest canopy, and belt out long, loud howls that can be heard several miles away. Some people say the howler's call sounds like a roaring lion. Others compare it to the sound of the whistle on a passing train. Either way, it's hard to imagine that such an incredible noise comes from animals that weigh between 8 and 17 pounds (3.6–7.7 kg).

Howler calls let rival monkey groups know where they are and warn them to stay away. The loud calling of two males or large choruses helps to strengthen the bonds among the howler monkeys. This is important because the adult members of a howler group aren't related to one another. When howlers are about 2 years old, they leave their parents' group and form new groups with other youngsters.

When a howler troop is satisfied that its loud morning calls have marked its territory, the monkeys climb down from the top of the canopy and begin to search for food. Howlers eat more leaves than any other kind of New World monkey. They also dine on fruit, seeds, and an occasional insect. These monkeys get most of the water they need from their food, but once in a while, they descend to the forest floor for a quick drink. Sometimes they eat a bit of soil. Dirt is a good source of important minerals that aren't found in plants.

Like woolly monkeys, howlers usually move slowly and cautiously through the trees. And like spider monkeys, they spend long periods of time resting. They are among the least active of the New World monkeys. Since howlers are often still, they can be difficult to spot—even though they are quite common in many areas.

A howler loudly greets the morning.

How do howlers produce such an impressive sound? Their **hyoid bone**—the bone supporting the tongue—is large and hollow. It opens into a very large **larynx**, or voice box, that can expand like a balloon. Together, these structures act like echo chambers, magnifying the sounds the monkeys produce.

A female howler mates for the first time when she is about 5 years old. When her baby is born, it has a silvery coat. Within a few days, the baby's coat begins to turn golden or reddish brown.

For the youngster's first month of life, it clings tightly to its mother. But then it learns to ride on her back, using its strong tail to stay balanced. Around the same time, the youngster begins to eat some solid food. When its mother is asleep, the little one may hop down and cautiously explore its surroundings or climb on its father. But as soon as its mother wakes up, the young howler scampers back to her side.

By the time the youngster is 6 months old, it spends a lot of time on its own. While the adults rest, young howlers play fight, chase one another through the trees, and practice hanging by their tails. Soon the youngsters will learn to survive on their own and wander off in search of a new group of friends.

SAKIS, BEARDED SAKIS, AND UAKARIS

SAKIS, BEARDED SAKIS, AND UAKARIS HAVE MANY THINGS IN common with capuchins and squirrel monkeys. They are about the same size, and they are lively and active for most of the day. It isn't hard to tell sakis and uakaris from their cousins, though. They have long, thick tails, and the shaggy hair covering most of their bodies makes them look larger than they really are. They also have odd-looking faces, as does the white-faced saki shown above.

Sakis live alone or in small, stable family groups. They spend most of their time looking for berries and other fruits, seeds, honey, leaves, and flowers. They also eat some birds and small mammals, including mice and bats. In the early afternoon, sakis take a brief rest and groom one another.

Only one female member of a saki group gives birth to young. The newborns usually arrive at the beginning of the wet season, when food is most abundant. The baby's mother provides most of its care, although its father sometimes holds and grooms the little one. As the baby grows, it spends more and more time playing with other group members.

When the youngster is about 4 months old, it can travel on its own. But it never strays far from its mother. She continues to share food with her youngster until it is about a year old, and she protects it from enemies. If a predator gets too close to the group, a saki mother hides her baby and runs away. Then she makes a lot of noise to lead the enemy away from her baby's hiding place.

A bearded saki looks similar to a saki, but it is a little smaller. Instead of having colorful hair on the sides of its face, it has a long, bristly beard. Bearded sakis have habits similar to sakis', but bearded sakis are usually found higher in the rain forest canopy. They eat mostly hard, unripe fruit and seeds, and they often supplement their diet with caterpillars.

Female bearded sakis usually give birth during the dry season. At first, the mother provides all the care. But when the baby is about 2 months old, other group members begin to groom and play with it. By the time the youngster is about 6 months old, it can travel short distances by itself. But it won't be ready to survive on its own for another 8 months.

A black-bearded saki uses its high-pitched whistle to communicate with other members of its group.

A white uakari looks like it's dressed for winter weather, but it lives in the hot, humid tropical forests of South America.

The red uakari gets its name from the color of its fur, not the color of its face. Uakaris stay in the trees during the wet season.

Uakaris are probably the strangest looking of the New World monkeys. They have bright red or dark black faces, and their heads are nearly bald. The shade of their bare faces changes with their moods. The rest of their bodies are covered with scruffy hair. These monkeys wag their short, bushy tails vigorously when they are excited.

Uakaris live in the lowland swampy forests around the Amazon River. During the wet season, when the land is flooded, uakaris never leave the trees. But during the short dry season, food and water are harder to find. The monkeys may climb down to the dry ground in search of seeds and young plant shoots. When uakaris find a puddle, they dip their furry hands into the water and suck it off the long strands of hair.

Most of the time, groups of 20 to 50 uakaris live and forage together. Each group consists of a few males, many females, and their young. All uakaris have strong teeth, which help them tear open hard fruits to reach the nutritious seeds inside. They also eat leaves, insects, and small mammals.

Like most monkeys, a uakari mother has one baby at a time. She devotes a great deal of time to feeding and protecting it. Many young uakaris continue to drink mother's milk until they are nearly 2 years old. It usually takes another year of care before they can survive on their own.

TITIS AND NIGHT MONKEYS

LIKE HOWLERS, TITIS START OFF EACH MORNING WITH long, loud calls that let other monkeys know where they are. Males and females mate for life and often belt out duets. Sometimes their youngsters also join in.

Titis, like the dusky titi shown above, live in tightly knit family groups. They travel and feed together all day long and sleep together at night. As titis forage in the Amazon forests of southeastern Brazil, the males are always in charge. It is their job to lead the group to fruit, leaves, insects, and other tasty treats. They also spend some time carrying newborns, so their mates get a chance to gather food.

In the morning, these fluffy-furred little creatures feed for several hours. When they stop to rest, family members sit side by side on a tree branch. They intertwine their long, thick tails and groom one another.

In the late afternoon, titis spend more time feeding. Then, just before dusk, they search for a place to spend the night. They huddle close, twist their tails together, and fall fast asleep.

Just as titis are drifting off to sleep, night monkeys are shaking themselves awake. They are the only monkeys that are active at night. Night monkeys look similar to titis, but they have much larger eyes. Their enormous eyes are specially designed to collect lots of light, so the monkeys can see in the dark.

On nights when the moon is a tiny sliver and the sky is dark, night monkeys move quietly through the rain forest. But when the moon is full, the little monkeys are bolder. They hoot and holler, twitter and sing to one another all night long. These noises help night monkeys stay in touch. They also scare away intruders.

In 1992, researchers, led by the Dutch scientist Marc van Roosmalen, discovered two new species of titi monkeys in Brazil. One is *Callicebus stephennashi.* It is silver with black and red markings and named after Stephen Nash, a well-known scientific illustrator. The other species is *Callicebus bernhardi.* It is named after Prince Bernhard of the Netherlands. The little monkey has a brownish gray body with a bright orange beard and a white-tipped tail.

Night monkeys have big eyes for seeing in the dark.

Like titis, night monkeys usually mate with the same partner year after year. The male is devoted to his family and plays a big role in raising the couple's youngsters. He carries the babies, plays with them, and protects them from enemies.

Since night monkeys don't have to worry about midday heat, they rarely take a break from foraging. This means they spend less time grooming.

Even though night monkeys sometimes fight, the disagreements usually don't last long. By the time day breaks, the monkey family is content to nestle inside a carefully chosen tree hole and fall asleep, with their long, bushy tails loosely intertwined.

A night monkey's favorite food is small, ripe fruit, but they also eat flowers, nectar, leaves, and insects.

CAN NEW WORLD MONKEYS SURVIVE?

ALTHOUGH NEW WORLD MONKEYS HAVE MANY predators, they have managed to survive on Earth for millions of years. Over time, each group—from marmosets to capuchins to titis—has developed its own unique ways of finding food and avoiding enemies. Night monkeys are active at night while their enemies are asleep. Capuchins harass predators until they give up and go away. Squirrel monkeys, shown above, give off a scent that few enemies can bear. Saki mothers often thrust themselves in harm's way to protect the babies they've carefully hidden nearby.

These strategies work well against natural predators, but New World monkeys are facing new enemies. Each year, human hunters kill many monkeys for food. Many more are captured and sold as pets. But the biggest threat of all is the loss of tropical rain forest lands.

In the last 30 years, more than 40 percent of the world's tropical forests have been destroyed. In some areas, most of the trees have been cut down for timber. In other places, entire forests have been burned so the land can be farmed.

Each year, another 27 million acres (11 million ha) are cleared. Experts predict that if the destruction continues, no tropical forests will be left in 50 years. Some monkey species may be able to survive, but a few are already in trouble.

Above: A roadside vendor offers to sell a capuchin monkey to a passing motorist in Managua, Nicaragua.
Left: Slash-and-burn methods destroy monkey habitat in the Amazon rain forests of Brazil.

The woolly spider monkey is an endangered species.

Woolly spider monkeys don't start having young until they are around 7 years old. They spend so much time raising each baby that they give birth just a few times during their lives. This is one reason why woolly spider monkeys are in danger of disappearing. Scientists estimate that only about four hundred of them exist in the wild.

Black lion tamarins are also facing **extinction.** In fact, scientists thought these little monkeys had died out completely. Then in 1970, a small population was discovered. These primates are protected by laws, and it is illegal to cut down their rain forest home. Still, only about one thousand exist in the wild. That may not be enough to make sure

black lion tamarins survive into the future.

Another species, the black-faced lion tamarin, was unknown to scientists until 1990. Both the monkeys and their home habitat are protected. But scientists aren't sure that the small population of 260 black-faced lion tamarins will be able to survive for long.

The good news is that people today understand the importance of rain forests and the creatures that call them home. Many groups are working hard to protect and preserve these unique environments. Let's hope it's not too late to save lion tamarins, woolly spider monkeys, and all the other monkeys that live in the Americas.

GLOSSARY

bands: in some New World monkeys, subgroups that forage together during the day and join a larger group at night

canopy: the top layer of a tropical forest

extinction: disappearing from Earth forever

forage: to search for food

groom: to pick insects, dirt, and bits of dead skin out of another animal's fur. For many animals, grooming is a way to express affection and establish trust.

habitats: areas where an animal or plant lives, grows, and reproduces

hominoids: the group of primates that includes the great apes and humans

hyoid bone: the bone that supports the tongue and related muscles

larynx: also called the voice box; a box-shaped structure in the throat that contains the vocal cords. It produces most of the sounds primates use to communicate.

mammals: animals that have backbones and fur and feed mother's milk to their young

New World monkeys: monkeys that live in southern Mexico, Central America, or South America

Old World monkeys: monkeys that live in Asia or Africa

opposable thumb: a thumb set opposite the other four fingers. Having hands with opposable thumbs makes it easier to grasp and hold food and other objects.

predator: an animal that hunts and kills other animals for food

prehensile: able to grasp and hold objects

prey: an animal that is hunted and killed for food

primates: the group of mammals that has arms and legs that can move freely, flexible fingers and toes, forward-facing eyes that can judge distances accurately, and large brains.

species: a group of living things that shares certain characteristics and can mate and produce healthy young

BIBLIOGRAPHY

Bower, Bruce. "The Secret Lives of Squirrel Monkeys." *Science News,* July 3, 1999.

De Roy, Tui. "Gremlins in a Fractured Forest: How the Fate of Elflike Marmosets and Lion Tamarins Is Tied to the Fortunes of a Fabled Piece of Brazil." *National Wildlife,* April–May 2002.

Dorfman, Andrea, and Michael D. Lemonick. "Monkeys Galore." *Time,* July 1, 2002.

Hershkovitz, Philip. *Living New World Monkeys.* Chicago: University of Chicago Press, 1977.

Kinzey, Warren G. *New World Primates: Ecology, Evolution, and Behavior.* New York: Walter de Gruyter, 1997.

Nowak, Robert M. *Walker's Mammals of the World.* 6th ed. Baltimore: Johns Hopkins University Press, 1999.

Personal observations, Costa Rica, February 2005.

WEBSITES

Conservation International

http://investigate.conservation.org/xp/IB/speciesdiversity/classifications/newworldmonkeys.xml

Conservation International provides information about the conservation of plants and animals around the world with photos and links to additional facts about specific habitats and living things.

New World Monkeys

http://anthro.palomar.edu/primate/prim_5.htm

This site contains descriptions of New World monkeys along with photos, a location map, and links to a pronunciation guide and glossary.

Rainforest Connection

http://rainforest.montclair.edu/pwebrf/rainforest.jsp

At this site, rain forest researchers in Panama reprort about life in the Central American rainforest to U.S. classrooms. Descriptions of New World monkeys are included in the Background section.

FURTHER READING

Dennard, Deborah. *Monkeys.* Minnetonka, MN: NorthWord, 2003.

Guiberson, Brenda Z. *Rain, Rain, Rain Forest.* New York: Holt, 2004.

Harman, Amanda. *New World Monkeys.* Danbury, CT: Grolier Educational Corporation, 2001.

Johnson, Rebecca L. *A Walk in the Rain Forest.* Minneapolis: Carolrhoda Books, Inc., 2001.

Martin, Patricia. *Monkeys of Central and South America.* New York: Children's Press, 2000.

Reid, Mary E. *Howlers and Other New World Monkeys.* Chicago: World Book, 2000.

Stewart, Melissa. *Sloths.* Minneapolis: Carolrhoda Books, Inc., 2005.

INDEX

ABOUT THE AUTHOR

In 2005, **Melissa Stewart** traveled to the Costa Rican rain forest with her family. Each morning, she was awakened by the long calls of howler monkeys. During the day, she saw dozens of spindly spider monkeys swinging through the trees in search of fruit. While cruising along the canals of Tortuguero National Park, she spotted a little capuchin snacking on a bright red pachira flower. All these firsthand observations helped Stewart write this book.

Before becoming a full-time writer, Stewart earned a bachelor's degree in biology from Union College, in New York state, and a master's degree in science and environmental journalism from New York University. She then spent a decade working as a science editor.

Stewart has written more than 70 children's books about animals, ecosystems, earth science, and space science. She has also contributed articles to *Ask, Click, Highlights for Children, National Geographic World, Northern Woodlands, Odyssey, Ranger Rick, Science World, Wildlife Conservation,* and *ZooGoer.* Stewart lives in Acton, Massachusetts. You can visit her website at www.melissa-stewart.com.

PHOTO ACKNOWLEDGMENTS

The images in this book are used with the permission of: © Brand X/SuperStock, all backgrounds on pp. 1, 5, 7, 9, 13, 14, 18, 21, 22, 27, 32, 33, 34, 38, 39, 41; © age fotostock/SuperStock, pp. 2–3, 14, 15 (main), 40, 43; © MaXx images/SuperStock, p. 4; © Gerry Lemmo, pp. 5, 12, 32, 33; © Suzanne Murphy-Larronde, p. 6 (left); © kevinschafer.com, pp. 6 (right), 30, 31; PhotoDisc Royalty Free by Getty Images, p. 7 (bottom); © Laura Westlund/Independent Picture Service, pp. 8, 18; © Claudia Adams/Root Resources, p. 9; Image Source Royalty Free by Getty Images, p. 10 (left); © CLAUS MEYER/Minden Pictures, p. 10 (right); © SuperStock, Inc./ SuperStock, pp. 11, 27; © Brand X/SuperStock, p. 13; © ZSSD/SuperStock, p. 15 (inset); © Petra Wegner/Alamy, p. 16; © Arco Images/Alamy, p. 17; © Terry Whittaker/Alamy, p. 19; © Fred Kamphues/SuperStock, p. 20; © Mauritius/SuperStock, p. 21; © PETE OXFORD/Minden Pictures, pp. 22, 23 (top); © Carlos Adolfo Sastoque N./SuperStock, pp. 23 (bottom), 35; © Gary Neil Corbett/SuperStock, p. 24 (inset); © GERARD LACZ/Animals Animals, p. 24 (main); © WERNER LAYER/Animals Animals, p. 25; © M. Lane/Peter Arnold, Inc., p. 26; © M. FOGDEN/OSF/Animals Animals, p. 28; © DANI/JESKE/Animals Animals, p. 29 (main); © Wegner P./Peter Arnold, Inc., p. 29 (inset); © Anthony Mercieca/SuperStock, p. 34; © Luiz C. Marigo/Peter Arnold, Inc., p. 36; © FABIO COLOMBINI MEDEIROS/Animals Animals, p. 37; © Ken Lucas/Visuals Unlimited, pp. 38, 39; © BIOS Denis-Huot M.&C./Peter Arnold, Inc., p. 41; © Nigel Smith/SuperStock, p. 42 (main); © Keith Dannemiller/CORBIS, p. 42 (inset).

Front Cover: © Tom and Pat Leeson.

Back Cover: © Brand X/ SuperStock.